# Cowboys of the Wild West

A cowboy separates a cow and her calf from the main herd.

# Cowboys of the Wild West

RUSSELL FREEDMAN

CLARION BOOKS
NEW YORK

Quotation permissions and photographic sources are cited on page 95.

Clarion Books
a Houghton Mifflin Company imprint
215 Park Avenue South, New York, NY 10003

Printed in the USA

Library of Congress Cataloging-in-Publication Data

Freedman, Russell.
Cowboys of the wild west.

Bibliography: p.    Includes index.
1. Cowboys—West (U.S.)—History—19th century—Juvenile
literature.    2. Frontier and pioneer life—West (U.S.)—
Juvenile literature.    3. West (U.S.)—Social life and
customs—Juvenile literature.    I. Title.
F596.F76   1985        978'.02        85-4200
ISBN 0-89919-301-3    PA ISBN 0-395-54800-4
HOR   20  19  18  17  16  15  14  13  12  11

*To Jim Kormier — my fellow tenderfoot*

# Contents

A Cow Herder on Horseback   9

Cowboy Clothes and Equipment   21

Roundup on the Open Range   35

Up the Trail   47

Ranch Life   65

The Last of the Old-Time Cowboys   79

Bibliography   93

Acknowledgments   95

Index   97

Texas trail-drivers. These cowboys from the XIT Ranch drove a herd of long-horns from Texas to Montana during the late 1880s. In Miles City, Montana, they went to a photographer's studio and posed proudly for this group portrait.

# A Cow Herder on Horseback

*I've roamed the Texas prairies,*
*I've followed the cattle trail;*
*I've rid a pitchin' pony*
*Till the hair come off his tail.*©

ACENTURY AGO, in the years following the Civil War, one million mustang ponies and ten million head of longhorn cattle were driven north out of Texas. Bawling and bellowing, the lanky longhorns tramped along dusty trails in herds that numbered a thousand animals or more.

Behind and beside and ahead of each herd rode groups of men on horseback. Often, they sang to the cattle as they drove them on. These old-time cow herders were mostly very young men, and in time they came to be known as cowboys.

Some were boys in fact as well as name. Youngsters still in their teens commonly worked as horse wranglers, caring for the saddle ponies that traveled with every trail outfit. A typical trail-driving cowboy was in his early twenties. Except for some cooks and bosses, there were few thirty-year-old men on the trail.

Cowboys drove great herds across wild prairies from Texas

to markets in Kansas and beyond. They swam the cattle across rivers and stayed with them during stampedes. A man spent eighteen hours a day in the saddle. At night he slept on the ground. Sometimes he lived on the trail for months with no comforts but a campfire and his bedroll.

At the end of the drive, the cattle were sold, the hands were paid off, and the trail outfit split up. Then the cowboys went into town to scrape off the trail dust and celebrate. Usually they stopped at the pineboard photographer's studio found in nearly every western cattle town. Decked out in their best duds and sporting the tools of their trade, they posed proudly for souvenir pictures to send to the folks back home. Some of those old photographs still survive. In them we can glimpse the cowboy as he really was, a hundred years ago.

The cowboy trade goes back more than four hundred years. It began in Mexico during the sixteenth century, when Spanish settlers brought the first domesticated horses and cattle to North America. Back home, the Spanish had kept their cattle penned up in pastures. But in the wide-open spaces of the New World, the cattle were allowed to wander freely, finding their own grass and water. The animals flourished. Soon, huge Spanish ranches were scattered across northern Mexico.

Since the cattle roamed far and wide, the ranchers needed skilled horsemen to look after their herds. They began to teach the local Indians to ride horses and handle cattle on the open range. These barefoot Indian cow herders were called *vaqueros*, from the Spanish word *vaca*, for cow. They were the first true cowboys, and they spent their days from sunrise to sunset in the saddle. They became experts at snaring a running steer with a braided rawhide rope, called *la reata* in Spanish. Over the years *la reata* — the lariat — became the cowboy's most important tool,

A Spanish vaquero

An early Texas cowboy

and the Mexican vaquero became a proud and independent ranch hand.

Vaqueros drove the first herds of cattle north into Texas early in the eighteenth century. By the time of the American Civil War (1861–1865), millions of hardy long-horned cattle were roaming the Texas plains. Many of these animals were descended from strays and runaways that had escaped from their owners, and they were as wild as buffalo or deer. They clustered together in small herds, hiding in thickets by day, running by night. If anyone tried to approach them on foot, they would paw the earth and toss their heads in anger.

Like most of the South, Texas was poor when the Civil War ended. Confederate money no longer had any value. The state's economy was in ruins. Yet longhorns were running wild all over the state.

Before the war, cattle had been raised mainly for their hides (for leather) and tallow, or fat (for candles and soap). Now, new methods of meat-packing and refrigeration had created a profit-

Beef on the hoof. A Texas longhorn.

able market for beef in the crowded cities of the North. Texas had plenty of beef on the hoof, but there were no railroads linking Texas with the rest of the country, where the beef was in demand. The only way to get the cattle to market was to walk them hundreds of miles north to the nearest railroad.

As Texas farmers and ranchers came home from the war, they began to organize what they called "cow hunts." By capturing wild longhorns and branding them as his own, a rancher could build up his herds and drive them north to be sold. Cow-hunters used the same methods to catch wild cattle that Mexican vaqueros had been using for a long time. They found a herd of longhorns by moonlight and fired a gun to make them stampede. Riding with the herd, they let the longhorns run for hours, until the cattle grew tired and slowed to a trot or walk. Then the men kept the animals moving for the next day or so, until the longhorns were so hungry and exhausted, they had tamed down and could be handled with ease.

Once the cattle had been caught and branded, they were set loose to graze until they were ready for market. Then they were rounded up and driven in large herds to Kansas railroad towns, where they were loaded aboard freight cars and shipped to meat-packing plants in Kansas City and Chicago.

As the demand for beef grew, the cattle-raising industry spread northward from Texas. New ranches began to spring up all across the northern plains, where only a few years before herds of buffalo had grazed. By the 1870s, most of the buffalo had been slaughtered. They were replaced by longhorn cattle brought up the trails from Texas. Soon, a vast tract of cattle country stretched from Colorado up through Wyoming, Montana, and the Dakotas.

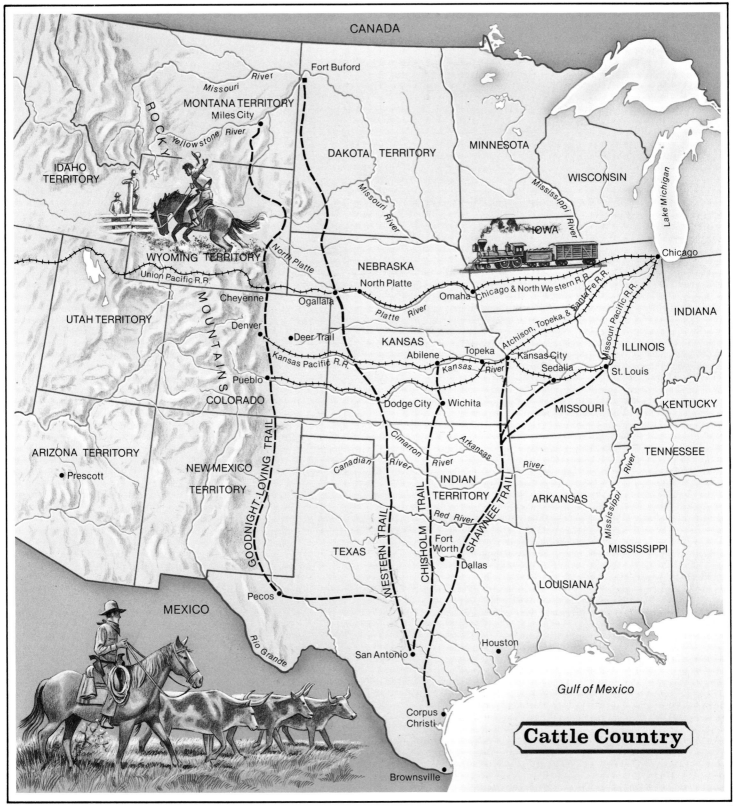

CANADA

Fort Buford

*Missouri* *River*

MONTANA TERRITORY
Miles City

IDAHO
TERRITORY

*Yellowstone* *River*

R O C K Y

DAKOTA TERRITORY

MINNESOTA

WISCONSIN

*Mississippi River*

Lake Michigan

WYOMING TERRITORY

IOWA

Chicago

Union Pacific R.R.

*North Platte*

NEBRASKA

North Platte

Omaha   Chicago & North Western R.R.

INDIANA

M
O
U
N
T
A
I
N
S

Cheyenne

Ogallala

*Platte* *River*

UTAH TERRITORY

Denver

Deer Trail

Atchison, Topeka, & Santa Fe R.R.

*Missouri Pacific R.R.*

ILLINOIS

KANSAS

Topeka

Kansas City

Kansas Pacific R.R.

Abilene

Sedalia

St. Louis

*Kansas* *River*

Pueblo

COLORADO

Dodge City   Wichita

MISSOURI

KENTUCKY

ARIZONA TERRITORY

Prescott

NEW MEXICO
TERRITORY

G
O
O
D
N
I
G
H
T
-
L
O
V
I
N
G

T
R
A
I
L

*Cimarron*   *River*

*Canadian* *River*

*Arkansas* *River*

TENNESSEE

INDIAN
TERRITORY

ARKANSAS

W
E
S
T
E
R
N

T
R
A
I
L

C
H
I
S
H
O
L
M

T
R
A
I
L

S
H
A
W
N
E
E

T
R
A
I
L

*Red* *River*

*Mississippi* *River*

MISSISSIPPI

TEXAS

Fort
Worth

Dallas

LOUISIANA

Pecos

MEXICO

*Rio Grande*

San Antonio

Houston

Gulf of Mexico

Corpus
Christi

**Cattle Country**

Brownsville

*Map by George Buctel*

At the heart of this booming cattle industry was the hardworking cowboy. Who was he, where was he from, and what was he like?

To begin with, most cowboys were Texans and other southerners, discharged soldiers back from the war. Jobs were scarce in the South, and the prospering cattle ranchers needed plenty of new hands. Along with the southerners, there were a number of mustered-out Union soldiers. Eventually, men and boys from many backgrounds and all parts of the country began to arrive in Texas, seeking jobs as cowhands. Some had been unlucky at home and were looking for a fresh start. Others were drawn to Texas because they had heard that a cowboy's life was adventurous and exciting.

Today, in movies and TV shows about the Old West, cowboys are usually white. In real life, they were often black or Mexican. Texas had been a slaveholding state before the Civil War. On Texas ranches, slaves broke horses and herded cattle. When the war ended, many freed slaves from Texas and other southern states went to work as professional cowhands. Most Texas trail outfits included black cowboys, and a few outfits were all black.

Mexican cowhands, descendants of the vaqueros, were common in southern Texas, where many ranches were still owned by old Spanish families. Other cowboys were American Indians, or had some Indian blood. In the Indian Territory (now Oklahoma), a number of cattle ranches were operated entirely by Native American cowboys.

In the movies, cowboys seem to spend a good part of their time chasing outlaws, battling Indians, rescuing the rancher's daughter, and hanging out in riotous cow towns like Abilene and

*Above:* Cowboys at mealtime, photographed in the Texas Panhandle around 1885. Black cowboys, such as the two men in this group, were a part of most Texas trail outfits. *Below:* Indian cowboys, photographed in the Cherokee Outlet (now Oklahoma) around 1890. These men are probably Caddo or Kickapoo Indians.

Dodge City. They wear huge white hats, skintight shirts, and shiny six-shooters slung low on each hip. That's not quite the way it was in the real Wild West.

A real cowboy was paid to herd cows. He spent most of his time rounding up longhorns, branding calves, and driving the herds to market. He was lucky if he made it into town twice in one year. Out on the range he wore practical work clothing, rode a horse owned by his employer, and seldom carried a gun. When he did, he wore it high and snug around his waist. He never carried two guns.

"There is one thing I would like to get straight," recalled an old-time cowboy named Teddy Blue Abbott. "I punched cows from '71 on [when he was ten years old], and I never yet saw a cowboy with two guns. I mean two six-shooters. Wild Bill carried two guns and so did some of those other city marshals, like Bat Masterson, but they were professional gunmen themselves, not cowpunchers. . . . A cowboy with two guns is all movie stuff, and so is this business of a gun on each hip."

Most cowboys were not sharpshooters, yet their work demanded exceptional skills. A cowboy had to be an expert roper and rider, an artist at busting broncs and whacking bulls. He had to know how to doctor an ailing cow or find a lost calf, how to calm a restless herd in the middle of the night, how to head off a thousand stampeding longhorns.

On a ranch, he worked ten to fourteen hours a day. On trail drives, he herded cattle from before dawn to after dusk, then spent two more hours on night guard duty. He had a tough, dirty, sweaty job, and often a dangerous one. He might be kicked by a horse, charged by a steer, trampled in a stampede, drowned

Working the herd

during a river crossing, or caught on the open prairie in the midst of an electrical storm. Probably more cowboys were killed by lightning than by outlaws or Indians. Riding accidents were the most common cause of cowboy deaths, followed by pneumonia.

Teddy Blue Abbott went up the trail for the first time in 1879, when he was eighteen years old. Sixty years later he recalled the men he had worked with: "In person the cowboys were mostly medium-sized men, as a heavy man was hard on horses, quick and wiry, and as a rule very good natured; in fact, it did not pay to be anything else. In character, their like never was or will be again. They were intensely loyal to the outfit they were working for and would fight to the death for it. They would follow their wagon boss through hell and never complain. I have seen them ride into camp after two days and nights on herd, lay down their saddle blankets in the rain and sleep like dead men, then get up laughing and joking about some good time they had in Ogallala or Dodge City. Living that kind of life, they were bound to be wild and brave."

Decked out in his best duds, a young cowboy poses before a painted back-drop in a Wyoming photographer's studio. The lariat is probably a studio prop.

# Cowboy Clothes and Equipment

*Oh, a ten-dollar hoss and a forty-dollar saddle,*
*And I'm goin' to punchin' Texas cattle.*©

A COWBOY OF THE 1860s would have had a hard time convincing a TV casting director that he was the real McCoy. As he rode across the range, he was wearing, more likely than not, the remnants of his Civil War uniform — flat-heeled marching boots, a gray Confederate army coat, and perhaps a floppy wool hat, its brim held up by thorns.

By the 1870s, a distinctive cowboy outfit had appeared on the range. This outfit changed over the years and differed from one region to the next, but it always identified the cowboy as surely as any uniform.

For their basic clothing, most cowboys wore the ordinary work clothes of the time — a loose-fitting shirt made of cotton or flannel and heavy-duty woolen pants. The pants might have buckskin sewn over the seat and down the inner thighs to keep them from wearing thin where they rubbed against the saddle. Levis didn't become popular until the 1890s, and at first they were dyed brown rather than blue.

On the range, cowboys needed practical, comfortable work clothes. The members of this roundup crew are wearing a variety of different hats, coats, vests, sweaters, shirts, and chaps.

Since it was difficult for a man on horseback to reach into his pants pockets, vests with deep pockets became standard cowboy gear. In the Southwest, many cowboys had heavy canvas jackets to protect their arms and bodies from thorns. On the northern plains, they had knee-length coats made of sheepskin or wool. Every cowboy had a slicker, or oilskin raincoat, rolled and tied behind his saddle.

To protect their legs while riding through mesquite and chaparral thickets, Mexican vaqueros had invented seatless leather leggings called *chaparreras,* or chaps. Early chaps, called "shotguns," were like heavy leather trousers that the cowboy stepped into. They were replaced by "batwing" chaps, which were cut

Chaps made of wool, leather, or fur protected a cowboy's legs in brushy country and in cold weather.

wider and wrapped around the leg to fasten in back. In the Southwest, chaps were usually made of smooth leather. In the North, cowboys sometimes wore "woolies," cold-weather chaps covered with wool or fur.

Cowboy boots were designed to fit the needs of a man on horseback. They had pointed toes so the rider could slip his foot easily into the stirrup, thin soles to give him the feel of the stirrup, and high heels to grip the stirrup firmly. True cowboy boots were almost knee-high, to keep out pebbles and dirt. They had floppy grips called "mule ears" to help the cowboy pull them on. He often tucked his trousers into his boot tops, so they would not get snagged on brush or tangled in the stirrups.

The fanciest boots were made of fine soft leather with lots of decorative stitching, which cowboys felt gave a snugger fit. Only the poorest or sloppiest cowboy was willing to wear ready-made boots. It was a matter of pride for a man to have his boots hand-made over his own special cast. A good pair of custom-made boots might cost a cowboy a month's wages.

Spurs were both useful working tools — they encouraged a horse to move quickly — and an important part of the cowboy's image. They came in many sizes and shapes, ranging from plain iron work spurs to elaborate silver dress spurs. Metal jinglebobs and heel chains created a musical accompaniment when a cowboy walked. If he swung his feet in just the right way, he could make the rowels on the spurs spin and ring against a wooden sidewalk with every step he took as he jingle-jangled along.

Another familiar cowboy trademark was a brightly colored bandanna, folded and tied around the cowboy's neck. The bandanna protected his neck from sunburn. During roundups and trail drives, it could be pulled over his face as a dust mask. In cold weather, it could be tied over his head to keep his ears warm. It came in handy as a sling, a bandage, or a tourniquet in case of snakebite. It could be used as a washcloth or a towel, or to blindfold and calm a skittish horse.

A cowboy's hat also served many useful purposes. The wide brim shaded his eyes from the sun, kept rain from running down his neck, and shielded his face from low-lying branches as he rode along. A hat could be used to fan a slow-starting campfire, to chase mosquitoes, or to carry water from a stream. Waved in the air, it was a signal that could be seen for a long distance. And it was useful for giving a pesky horse a slap on the rump.

At a roundup camp in Colorado, cowboys get together to show off their spurs.

Cowboy hats differed from one region of the country to another. In the Southwest, the hat had a tall crown and a wide brim to offer maximum protection from the desert sun. On the windy northern plains, the brims were narrower and the crowns lower so the hat would not blow away. An experienced cowhand could guess a stranger's home range simply by looking at his hat.

An expensive dress hat was a cherished possession. The brim might be braided with silk, laced with leather, or studded with silver. The hatband might be made of gold or silver wire, or from the dressed skin of a diamondback rattlesnake. To a fashion-conscious cowboy, a fine hat with a fancy sweatband was just as important as an expensive pair of boots.

Cowboys liked to dress up as much as anyone. On the range they wore practical work clothes, but for special occasions they put on the best clothes they could afford. When eighteen-year-old Teddy Blue finished his first long trail drive in 1879, he bought himself a new outfit: "Before I went home, I stopped in North Platte, where they paid us off, and bought me some new clothes. . . . I had a white Stetson hat that I paid ten dollars for and new pants that cost twelve dollars, and a good shirt and fancy boots. They had colored tops, red and blue, with a half-moon and star on them. Lord, I was proud of those clothes! They were the kind of clothes top hands wore, and I thought I was dressed right for the first time in my life. I believe one reason I went home was just so I could show them off."

In old photographs of cowboys taken out on the range, often there are no firearms in sight. Cowboys did carry weapons in the early days, right after the Civil War, when outlaws and hostile Indians were more of a threat than later on. By the late 1870s, however, the frontier had quieted down and working cowboys seldom kept their guns with them. In fact, many Texas counties and several Kansas cattle towns passed pistol laws that prohibited the carrying of side arms unless you were an officer of the law.

Besides, it was dangerous and uncomfortable to work cattle on horseback with a loaded pistol hanging from your hip or a rifle strapped to your saddle. A Colt .45 — the popular six-shooter — had an eight-inch barrel and weighed two-and-a-half pounds. A rifle carried in a saddle scabbard rubbed against the horse, causing painful sores. On roundups and trail drives, cowboys usually stashed their guns and rifles in the supply wagon or back at the bunkhouse.

Rifles and shotguns were used most commonly for hunting game. A six-shooter was useful for killing rattlesnakes, putting a crippled horse or cow out of its misery, or turning aside a stampede when fired just past the leaders' heads. Three gun shots evenly spaced were a universal distress signal. Cowboys also liked to show off with their six-shooters, firing at random targets or into the air. But most cowboys were not sharpshooters. They had little time for target practice, and ammunition was expensive.

They spent lots of time practicing with their lariats, however. With his lariat, a 150-pound cowhand could capture a 1,000-pound steer. Every cowboy knew how to throw a lariat so that the running loop at one end would snare a cow's horns, a horse's neck, or the hoofs of either.

Roping a calf

The lariat was an essential tool during roundups, brandings, and cattle drives. Made of tough, twisted plant fiber or braided rawhide, it could be anywhere from thirty to sixty feet long. With practice, almost anyone could learn to throw a lariat while standing on the ground. But it took considerable skill to do the same thing from the back of a galloping horse that was chasing a twisting, dodging steer.

A cowboy's saddle was another essential piece of equipment. Since he spent most of his waking hours in his saddle, it had to

A cowboy, who was seldom seen without his hat, was especially proud of owning a fine saddle.

be comfortable. And it had to be ruggedly built to withstand plenty of hard wear. Strangers could judge a man's standing in the cowboy trade by the make and condition of his saddle. If it was built well and maintained with care, a cowboy could ride for hours without making his horse uncomfortable or sore.

A saddle weighed between thirty and forty pounds. It was made from a carved wooden frame covered with leather. At the front of the saddle was a horn, used to secure the lariat when the cowboy roped a steer. The cowboy's legs hung down over leather flaps called "fenders." His boots rested on broad wooden or metal stirrups. He could stand in the stirrups while riding down a steep slope or trotting along the trail. The "cinch" went around the horse's body and under its belly, holding the saddle in place. Long leather ties were used to attach bedrolls, rain slickers, and other gear.

A fine saddle, handmade by a master craftsman in a western town, could cost more than a month's pay. A cowboy might be willing to risk losing his custom-made boots, his silver spurs, or his best Stetson on the outcome of a horse race or some other sporting event, but he would part with his saddle only in the most desperate circumstances. To say of a cowboy, "He's sold his saddle," meant that he was quitting the cowboy trade for good.

Every cowboy owned his saddle, but he did not always own a horse. Horses were furnished by the ranch or trail outfit he was working for. If he had a horse, he kept it with the ranch's common pool of horses as long as he was employed there. Usually, he was given the use of perhaps six or eight horses by the rancher or trail boss who hired him. Saddle horses were ridden hard, and a man

Broncobusting. A cowboy teaches a wild horse to wear the saddle and obey his commands.

might change mounts several times a day. As long as a cowboy stayed with an outfit, the string of horses assigned to him were his, as surely as if he did own them. If a boss wanted a man to quit, he would take the cowboy's favorite horse away from him. That always meant that the cowboy should leave of his own accord before he had to be fired.

Most of these horses were mustang ponies, which ran wild on the western plains. A hardy breed—small, tough, and fast—they were captured and tamed by both the Plains Indians and by white settlers in the West. Cowboys preferred them to the larger horses imported from the East. "Beautiful little creatures they were—generally cream, buckskin, or mouse-colored," recalled a Texas cowboy named James Cook. "As a rule they were clean-limbed, and their hoofs were black and perfect. No blacksmith

or hoof-shaper had ever tinkered with their feet or forced them to wear iron shoes, and their hoofs would stand wear over the roughest trails. They required no grain, but rustled food for themselves."

Mustangs came from open rangeland, where they roamed free until about the age of four. Every spring, these four-year-olds were captured, driven to corrals, then tamed to the saddle and trained. Taming was called "breaking" or "busting," which meant that the animal's wild spirit was literally "broken" as the horse learned to fear, respect, and obey its rider. A broncobuster might be any local cowboy who was a good rider, or he might be a professional buster who traveled from ranch to ranch.

There was no easy way to break a wild bronco that had never been ridden before. The struggling horse was roped, tied to a

A professional broncobuster at work

post, and bridled. After the bridle came the saddle blanket, the saddle, and then the rider. With his spurs, his quirt (a short whip), and his rope end, the broncobuster beat in the lesson that disobedience brings instant punishment. No matter how violently the horse kicked and bucked, the buster would break its spirit and ride it to a standstill.

Once broken, the horse was trained to help its rider handle cattle. A clever horse was said to have "cow sense." Horses with special talents or abilities were favored for certain jobs. A good distance horse had long legs, lots of endurance, and an easy gait. A horse used for night herding had to have keen eyesight, a sure sense of direction, and a calm disposition.

"On warm moonlit nights as I rode around the herd, I would say to myself, 'This is the life!'" James Cook remembered. "My horse seemed to understand my thoughts, and to share my feeling. I always picked the best horse in my string for my night animal, and used him whenever I had to night herd. He and I became real friends. When I was in a merry mood he seemed to feel the same way, and on dark and stormy nights when the cattle were ready to jump and stampede at any minute and everyone was keyed up, I could feel him trembling under me; occasionally when we stood still, I could hear his heart thumping with excitement."

Pressing home the branding irons

# Roundup on the Open Range

*A cowboy's life is a dreary, dreary life,*
*Some say it's free from care;*
*Rounding up the cattle from morning till night*
*In the middle of the prairie so bare.*©

I N THE DAYS BEFORE fences separated one ranch from the next, the prairie was wide-open to everyone. Ranchers simply turned their cattle loose and let them graze as they wished.

During the year, the cattle wandered off in all directions, sometimes by ones and twos, sometimes in bunches. As they roamed miles from their home range, they mixed and mingled with cattle from other ranches, unmindful of who owned them. Twice a year, in the spring and again in the fall, roundups were held throughout the ranching country to gather these widely scattered longhorns and sort them out.

"The busiest time on a ranch is the preparation for the spring roundups," said a Texas cowhand. "There are saddles to mend, hobbles to make, grub wagons to overhaul and horses to get in shape, shoeing and trimming up, quirts to make, ropes to straighten up, and planning till you can't rest."

A roundup camp in Colorado during the 1880s

In many ways, a roundup resembled a military campaign. Cowboys from neighboring ranches worked together to hunt down all the cattle in a particular district. A really big spring roundup might cover hundreds of square miles, last for several weeks, and involve three or four hundred cowboys from a dozen different ranches.

A few days before the roundup was to start, chuck wagons drawn by teams of mules began to arrive at a chosen meeting place. They were followed by groups of cowboys coming from all directions, driving herds of saddle ponies. While waiting at the campground for everyone to show up, the cowboys had a chance to wander from wagon to wagon, greeting old friends, swapping stories with strangers, playing poker, mumble-the-peg, chuck-a-luck, fuzzy-guzzy and other games of amusement and chance. Once the roundup got under way, there would be no time to relax. The men would work from dawn to dusk and never get enough rest.

A roundup always followed a carefully worked-out plan. Each

Roping a horse from the remuda

squad of cowboys was assigned to a single chuck wagon. These men worked one range at a time, flushing out all the cattle in that area and gathering them together for sorting, counting, and branding. When that range had been covered, the squad with its chuck wagon moved on to the next range.

The day's work started long before sunup as the cook rattled his pots and pans and shouted something like, "Rise and shine! Grub pile! Come a-runnin', boys!" The drowsy cowboys would climb out of their bedrolls, pull on their pants and boots, splash their faces with cold water, and have a quick breakfast of pancakes, bacon, and strong black coffee around the glowing campfire.

As the men ate, the horse wrangler was bringing up the outfit's band of saddle ponies, called the *remuda* (from a Spanish word meaning "replacement" or "change"). Each man had his own string of horses in the remuda, so he could change mounts during the day. The wrangler collected the horses from their night pasture and drove them into a rope corral close by the chuck wagon. As the ponies milled about and dodged, each cowboy roped and saddled his morning horse. At the first light of dawn, the men moved out.

The cook packed up his gear and soon he was ready to move out, too. He climbed into the high seat of his chuck wagon, cracked his whip over the heads of the mules, and rumbled off, followed by the horse wrangler and the remuda. They headed for a roundup ground several miles away, which would be the center of the day's work.

The cowboys, meanwhile, were fanning out across the range. Every two miles or so, a rider would peel off from the group, ready to search his assigned area for cattle. By the middle of the morning, the riders had formed a circle perhaps twenty miles across, with the roundup ground at the center of the circle. As the men began to find cattle, they drove them in toward the roundup ground.

A cowboy named Hiram Craig has described a Texas roundup during the 1880s: "The men, so sent out, all going in different directions, formed a veritable spider's web, with the roundup grounds in the center. As soon as the boys would 'whoop 'em up,' the cattle were on the run, and would make for the grounds. There was little danger or chance for any cattle escaping, as when they would leave the path of one man they would drift into the path of the next man, and the nearer they came to the grounds, the more men would come in sight – finally forming one big herd, and then the fun would start."

In flat country, it was simple enough to find the cattle. But in broken country, the cowboys had to look behind every hill, poke into every thicket, gulley, and ravine. Their horses skidded down steep-sided cutbanks and washouts and jumped from ledge to ledge as they spooked reluctant cows from their hiding places and sent them trotting across the prairie toward the roundup ground.

A man standing by the chuck wagon in the middle of the roundup ground could see clouds of dust appear far out on the range as the cowboys drove the cattle before them. Small bunches of running cattle began to merge together, until all the animals were concentrated into one milling herd. The cowboys whistled and yelled and moved their horses in close to keep defiant cows from breaking out of the herd.

Once the cattle had calmed down and started to graze, the cowboys took time off for dinner, their midday meal. They filed past the cookfire to have their tin plates heaped with food. A roundup crew usually ate well. By tradition, the rancher whose

Cowboys eating dinner by their chuck wagon. An iron pot hangs over an open cook fire at the far left. The young boy is probably the horse wrangler.

land was being worked that day had butchered one of his own steers. The cook had barbecued the meat over an open fire, serving it up with hot biscuits and potatoes, and often with puddings and pies he had prepared that morning. After the meal, each man scraped his plate and threw it into the wooden washtub by the chuck wagon. Then he went over to the rope corral where the wrangler was holding the remuda and caught a fresh horse for the afternoon's work.

The afternoon was spent sorting out the cattle and branding new calves. Most of the cattle rounded up on any one day belonged to the ranch where the cowboys happened to be working. But there were always quite a few cows that had strayed over from neighboring ranches, so the animals had to be sorted out according to owner, and the new calves had to be branded with the owner's special mark. During a big roundup, when cattle from several ranches were mixed together in the herds, each ranch had a representative on the scene with a tally book to record all the calves branded for his employer.

Certain horses were especially trained for cutting, or separating, cows and their calves from the rest of the herd. Cutting required close cooperation between a cowboy and his horse. First the cowboy would pick out a cow accompanied by her unbranded calf. He would ride quietly into the herd without upsetting the cattle, turn his horse toward the cow he had singled out, and nudge her gently away from the rest of the herd as her calf followed on her heels.

A smart cutting horse knew just what to do. Once the horse understood which cow its rider was after, it would never take its eyes off that cow. If the cow tried to escape, the horse would stay close behind her, dodging and twisting when she did, nipping at her heels. When the cow and her calf were finally outside the herd, the horse would stay between them and the rest of the herd, so they could not run back in.

The next step was to rope the calf, drag it to the branding fire, and burn its mother's brand into its flank. This was a tricky job, since a cow loves her calf and will try to protect it. As the cowboy approached on his horse, the cow would stand in front of her calf, moaning in alarm and displaying her horns. Sometimes she would try to attack.

The cowboy maneuvered into position. Swinging his lariat over his head, he sent it flying toward its target, dropping the loop over the calf's head, then jerking the rope tight around the animal's neck. Then he pulled the stiff-legged, resisting calf across the roundup ground to the branding fire.

If a calf was already very close to the fire, the cowboy might use a sidearm motion to throw his lariat, roping the calf by its hind legs, jerking it to the ground, then dragging it to the fire side-up and ready for branding. If the calf had been head-roped, it had to be wrestled to the ground.

Waiting in the dust and heat by the branding fire were cowboys called "flankers." As a calf was dragged up, one or two flankers would rush over, grab the calf by its flanks, knock its legs out from under it, then quickly flip the animal up and out so that it landed on its side. Then the frightened, winded calf was pinned to the ground. One man held down its head, another grabbed its hind legs and pulled them back to stretch its skin, while a third ran up with the red-hot branding iron. He pressed the iron home as the little animal bawled in panic and pain.

Displaying her horns, a cow tries to protect her roped calf.

A resisting calf is dragged across the roundup ground to the branding fire.

Two "flankers" lift a roped calf...

and flip it over.

Before branding, a calf has to be wrestled to the ground and pinned down.

Often, as one man branded a calf, another would use a sharpened pocket knife to cut a notch in its ear. The shape and position of the ear notch served as an additional way of identifying the animal. As soon as the calf was released, it would scramble to its feet and shake its head, splattering blood in all directions. Then it would run off, looking for its mother. By that time, another calf was being dragged to the fire.

An experienced crew could brand more than one hundred calves an hour. The air was filled with dust and with white smoke from burning hair and flesh. The cowboys had to shout to be heard over the commotion of calves bawling for their mothers and cows bellowing for their calves.

"This was all done on the open prairie," Hiram Craig remembered. "We made our fires to heat the branding irons, would rope the calves or cattle, as the case may be, on horseback, drag them to the fire and put the brand on them. It was also the duty of the roundup boss to see that no large calf was cut out of the roundup herd unless it was accompanied by its mother. The roundup boss had to act somewhat in the capacity of a judge. He had to see that all disputes were satisfactorily settled. If trouble arose regarding the ownership of an animal the roundup boss would find out what brand each one of the disputing parties were claiming the animal under, and if they could come to no agreement, the animal was roped, the brand moistened with water to make it plainer, or he would shear the hair off where the brand was located, and in that way determine the ownership. All this was done immediately, and then the work would proceed. . . . The whole roundup was conducted in a strictly business way, and such a thing as 'red tape' was unknown."

A roundup went on day after day until all the cattle in the district had been accounted for. Every morning the chuck wagon moved to a new roundup ground, as cowboys swept the surrounding area clear of cattle. Every afternoon the cattle were sorted, counted, and branded. Animals that belonged on that particular range were set free to graze. Strays were gathered together to be returned to their home ranges. Animals ready for market were kept in a separate herd, so they could be driven north and sold.

A trail herd traveling from Hale County, Texas, to Montana Territory in 1882.
At the right of the photograph, the wrangler is driving the remuda of horses.
Behind them, the herd of longhorns stretches out along the trail.

# Up the Trail

*What keeps the herd from running,*
*Stampeding far and wide?*
*The cowboy's long, low whistle,*
*And singing by their side.*©

O N ITS HOME RANGE in Texas, a four-year-old longhorn was worth maybe three or four dollars. Up north, the same animal might fetch as much as forty dollars. Since there were no railroads leading to Texas, the cattle had to be put on the trail and marched north.

It took two or three months to drive a herd from Texas to railroad shipping points in Kansas. It took as long as six months to deliver cattle to ranches in Wyoming, Montana, or the Dakotas, where they would fatten on the rich grasses of the northern plains before being sent to the slaughterhouse.

Cowboys who took part in the great trail drives of the 1860s, 1870s, and 1880s would talk about the experience for the rest of their lives. Cattle panicked during river crossings and stampeded without warning in the dark of the night. Settlers armed with shotguns tried to drive the herds from their fields. There was always the chance of trouble with outlaws or Indians. And when a storm struck the open prairie, the men had no shelter to hide under. "Last night we had another of those miserable nights," one trail driver wrote in his diary. "Rain poured down. Beeves ran. Wind blew. Was on my horse the whole night."

Several trails led north from Texas. The most popular was the Chisholm Trail, a wide and dusty pathway that offered plenty of grass and good water holes all along the route. Beaten down by millions of clumping hoofs, eroded by rain and wind, the trail gradually sank into the ground, until it was lower than the plains it crossed.

A typical trail drive might involve two or three thousand head of cattle, perhaps sixty or seventy horses, and ten or twelve cowhands. The man in charge of the outfit, the trail boss, was hired by the owner of the cattle to drive the herd to market. He had to

Texas cattle moving north

make sure that the longhorns got enough grass and water and did not lose weight during the drive. He decided how far the outfit would travel each day and where it would stop to bed down for the night. He negotiated with Indians and with white settlers who objected to the herds crossing their land. And he supervised his crew. A trail boss earned about $100 a month.

The cook was sometimes an older man, often an ex-cowboy. He drove the chuck wagon, which carried the outfit's food and equipment. It was his job to set up camp every night, to fix three hot meals a day, and to care for his wagon and the mules that pulled it. He also served as a medic for the men and their horses, fixing up cuts and bruises, dealing with broken bones and fevers right on the trail. The cowboys took their orders from the trail boss, but a good cook was the key to a contented trail crew. He was paid between $35 and $50 a month.

Every trail outfit also included a horse wrangler, who was in charge of the remuda, or band of saddle ponies. He was usually the youngest member of the outfit, a boy who was old enough to do a man's work. He drove the horses by day, found a pasture for them at night, and rounded them up several times a day so the cowboys could change mounts. The wrangler also worked as the cook's helper and clean-up boy. He earned perhaps $25 a month, while the regular hands received around $30.

The chuck wagon carried everything a crew of ten or twelve men would need during a journey lasting several months. Strapped to one side of the wagon was a big wooden water barrel, to the other a heavy tool box. Slung under the wagon like a hammock was a dried cowhide called the "caboose," which carried kindling

Moving camp. The men's bedrolls—feather comforters covered by canvas tarpaulins—are ready to be loaded into the wagon.

wood. The bed of the wagon held cooking utensils, an ax and shovel, ropes and stake pins, and the men's bedrolls. At the rear of the wagon, facing aft, was the chuck box with its hinged lid that folded down onto a swinging leg, making a worktable for the cook. Inside the chuck box were many drawers, cubbyholes, and compartments holding such items as coffee, sugar, bacon, beans, flour, and salt, along with medicines like castor oil and horse liniment.

On the trail, the chuck wagon was the center of a cowboy's

A chuck wagon moves on to the next campground.

world. At mealtimes, the men sat on the ground near the wagon while they ate. At night, they rolled their bedrolls in a tight circle around the wagon. Meals tended to be monotonous, with lots of boiled beans, fried bacon, biscuits, black coffee, and dried apples or prunes. Even though they were surrounded by beef cattle, the men did not often eat beef during a trail drive. Killing a steer on the trail was wasteful, since only a small part of the meat could be eaten before it spoiled.

The cook was always the first man awake in the morning.

When breakfast was ready, he shouted for the rest of the crew to get up. A short distance away, the cattle were still sleeping on their bed-ground, watched by the two cowboys on the last guard. They stayed with the herd while the other hands gulped hot black coffee from tin cups in the predawn darkness.

At daybreak, the cattle began to stir. They rose swiftly to their feet and were allowed to graze for a while before the day's drive began. The night guards were relieved by two other men so they could have breakfast. The wrangler, meanwhile, had driven

A cook works at his chuck box.

the remuda to a rope corral near the chuck wagon, where the cowboys caught and saddled their morning horses. The men tied up their bedrolls and tossed them into the back of the wagon. The cook cleared away his pots and pans and hung them back in place. Then he climbed into his wagon and headed up the trail to help the trail boss pick out a good spot for a midday camp.

The grazing longhorns had already drifted a couple of miles north. Now it was time to turn them onto the trail. The cowboys began to squeeze the bawling cows into a long ragged line of march. Men rode back and forth along the edges of the strung-out herd, chasing strays and shouting, "Ho cattle! Ho ho ho!" Soon the animals were tramping along in regular formation, led by a few steers who marched to the head of the herd every morning and stayed there. The cows and calves fell in behind them, each animal finding the same position in line every day. No matter how scrambled the cattle became when they bedded down for the night, they would always seek out their rightful places in the line when the drive began the next morning.

The cowboys rode in formation, too. Up front were the pointers, two men in the lead who pointed the steers in the right direction and set the pace. Behind them, on either side of the herd, came the swing riders and flank riders, who patrolled the line of march and kept the cattle from wandering too far out from the herd. The drag riders rode at the end of the line, bandannas pulled over their noses and mouths as they caught all the dust of the trail. They kept the slowest animals from straggling behind. Since the drag was the worst position, most trail bosses tried to rotate their men during the day. "I've seen drag riders come off herd

Drag riders

with the dust half-an-inch deep on their hats and thick as fur in their eyebrows," said Teddy Blue Abbott. "If they shook their head or you tapped their cheek, the dust would fall off them in showers."

At noon, the outfit stopped at the camping ground picked out earlier that morning by the trail boss. The cattle grazed while the men ate dinner and rested. After an hour or so, they were back on the trail.

The trail seemed to stretch endlessly northward, a wide chocolate band cutting across vast expanses of prairie. Far off in the distance, the cowboys could see purple mountain ranges shimmering in the haze of the afternoon heat. The cattle's hoofs thudded along the hard-packed earth and their horns clattered as they swung their heads. It was important to keep the herd quiet and moving at a steady pace. If they were driven too fast, they would lose weight during the drive and would bring a lower price. On a good day, a herd would travel maybe fifteen or twenty miles.

Just before sundown, the cattle were turned off the trail at a bed-ground near the outfit's night camp, where the cook was already fixing supper. As the longhorns grazed, two cowboys circled the herd on horseback, riding around and around in the twilight until the drowsy cows were gathered into a compact herd and were ready to lie down for the night.

At the campfire nearby, the men ate their supper and laid out their billowy bedrolls — quilts covered over with big tarps. They chatted quietly in the gathering darkness, trading yarns, telling jokes, talking about the day's events. One of the men might play his harmonica or fiddle. But the cowboys rarely stayed up late. Because of night guard and early rising, a man could never get more than six hours sleep.

There were usually four watches at night. On each watch, two men would ride slowly around the sleeping cattle, moving in opposite directions, humming, whistling, or singing softly to the longhorns, as a mother croons to her baby. The cows seemed to be calmed by the sound of a human voice. Traditional cowboy songs were lullabies, meant to quiet restless cattle at night. Many of the songs were slow and sentimental, taking their rhythm from a horse's gait as it tiptoed around a sleeping herd.

Changing the night guard. Some of these men are preparing to go on guard duty, while others are bedding down.

Cowboys also sang on the trail, and for the same reason — to reassure the cattle. Some songs were composed on the spot, while others had familiar verses that all cowboys knew. "The trail boss would never pick on [employ] a fellow that couldn't sing and whistle, and we boys would consider it a dull day's drive if we didn't add at least one verse," recalled a Texas cowhand named J. M. Grigsby. "And bad, dark nights, the cowboy that could keep up the most racket [sing the best] was the pet of the bunch."

Longhorns were a scary lot, and bad, dark nights were stampede time. Almost any noise or disturbance — a flash of lightning, a rabbit moving through the brush, a cowboy striking a match — could panic a herd and send it into wild flight. The sleeping cowboys would be awakened by the rumbling of hoofs and the ground trembling beneath their bedrolls.

All hands would leap from their beds, dash to their night horses, and gallop into the dark. The fastest riders would overtake the leaders of the stampede and try to turn them from their course. If the cattle refused to turn, the men would fire their six-shooters close to the leaders' ears or slap slickers at their faces. When the leaders finally did turn, the cowboys forced the stampeding herd to start moving in a wide circle, to wind in upon itself like a spring until the cattle began to bunch up and mill about. Only then would the stampede come to an end.

"Stampedes were something frightful to see, and any man's knees will rattle when the big longhorns start to run," recalled a cowboy named Jim Herron. "There was nothing to do then but run with them, stay ahead of them if you could, and turn them into a tight mill when you got the chance, circle them until they was wound up tight as an eight-day clock on Sunday. It took the best night horse to stay with them. Once, we rode alongside the leaders for five miles, then gathered cattle over that five-mile stretch all the next day."

Cowboys trying to stop a stampede were always in danger. As they galloped through darkness and dust, they could not see the ground ahead of them, their fellow hands, or even most of the herd. The land was pockmarked with badger and prairie-dog holes, crisscrossed by cuts and gullies that could trip a galloping horse and send its rider sprawling. The greatest danger came when the cattle began to circle and mill, for then the animals were so jammed together a man might be jostled from his horse and trampled underfoot. If a cowboy fell from his horse into a milling herd, there was seldom anything left to bury.

River crossings could also be perilous. Moving north from Texas, a herd had to cross a half-dozen wide, muddy rivers. Often the cattle could wade across. If not, they had to plunge in and swim, with just their horns and noses showing above the water. During a crossing, cows might be trapped by beds of quicksand or caught in submerged tangles of driftwood. A single animal stumbling and struggling to regain its footing could cause a panic in midstream. Cattle and horses would thrash wildly about, pushing each other under in the confusion. The cowboys struggled to untangle the terrified animals and get them moving in the right direction.

The Red River marked the boundary between the state of Texas and the Indian Territory, land that had been set aside by the United States government for Indian tribes forced to move there from other parts of the country. This region had been guaranteed to the Indians forever by treaty. They raised their

Crossing a river

own cattle on the grasslands of the Indian Territory, and they regarded the white trail-drivers and their huge herds as illegal trespassers.

A number of tribes demanded that the trail-drivers pay tolls for the cattle crossing their land and eating their grass. On the old Shawnee Trail, the Cherokees charged a toll of ten cents a head and ran an efficient police patrol called the Cherokee Light Brigade to see that the tolls were paid.

Often a trail boss would offer the Indians a few head of cattle as payment, then go on his way in peace. Occasionally, trouble broke out. Some trail bosses refused to pay any tolls at all and tried to scare the Indians off with threats or gunplay. The Indians, in turn, would creep toward an encampment at night, stampede the cattle by leaping up and waving blankets at them, then make off with as many of the scattered animals as they could catch.

The Comanches of Texas — proud warriors and superb horsemen — became a serious hazard on the Goodnight-Loving Trail, which ran west across Texas, then turned north into New Mexico

The last job of a trail drive was to load the cattle aboard railroad stockcars. Because they used long metal-tipped poles to prod the longhorns, the men began to call themselves "cowpunchers" or "cowpokes."

and Colorado. They had been waging war against European invaders for nearly two hundred years, fighting first the Spaniards and later the Texans, who had taken their best hunting grounds. During the 1860s and early 1870s, Comanche warriors would charge over a hill and attack trail-driving outfits head on, stealing horses and running off entire herds. By the late 1870s, however, most of the hostile tribes in the West had been defeated and subdued by United States government troops. From then on, trail-drivers had more to fear from lightning and stampedes than from angry Indians.

A trail drive always had some exciting moments, but mostly the long journey north was monotonous and uneventful — mile after mile of dust, heat, blisters, and boredom. The men were happy to see the end of the trail.

Once they had reached Wichita, Abilene, Dodge City, or some other Kansas cattle town where the railroad ended, the cows were crowded into big holding pens and sold. Then they were loaded aboard railroad freight cars and shipped east to meet their fate in the slaughterhouses of Kansas City or Chicago. Often the saddle ponies were sold too, along with the chuck wagon and other trail gear. The men were paid off, and the trail outfit disbanded.

Grimy and bearded, the cowboys headed straight for town, eager to relax and let off steam. For months they had worked hard, slept little, and worn the same smelly clothes day after day. Now they could soak lazily in steaming rooming-house bathtubs, get themselves haircuts and shaves, sleep on clean sheets, eat at real tables, splurge on new clothes, and celebrate their freedom from the trail with a wild, foot-stomping night on the town.

The main street of Dodge City, Kansas, in 1878—a familiar sight to the trail-drivers of Texas

A cowboy might earn anywhere from fifty to ninety dollars in wages during a trail drive to Kansas. Money went fast along the rough streets of the booming cattle towns, vanishing like magic in the saloons, dance halls, gambling parlors, and shops. When a cowhand was tired of celebrating, or had spent most of his hard-earned cash, he would head south, find work on a ranch, then go up the trail again the following year.

G. O. Burrows made many trips up the trail and returned to Texas every time: "I always had the 'big time' when I arrived in good old Santone [San Antonio] rigged out with a pair of high-heeled boots and striped breeches, and about $6.30 worth

"DANCE-HOUSE."

At the end of the trail

of other clothes. Along about sundown you could find me at Jack Harris' show occupying a front seat and clamoring for the next performance. This 'big time' would last but a few days, however, for I would soon be 'busted' and have to borrow money to get out to the ranch, where I would put in the fall and winter telling about the big things I had seen up north. The next spring I would have the same old trip, the same old things would happen in the same old way, and with the same old wind-up. I put in eighteen or twenty years on the trail, and all I had in the final outcome was the high-heeled boots, the striped pants and about $4.80 worth of other clothes, so there you are."

A cattle ranch on the Cimarron River

# Ranch Life

*I am a wandering cowboy,*
*From ranch to ranch I roam;*
*At every ranch when welcome,*
*I make myself at home.*©

MOST COWBOYS A century ago were wandering cowboys. Always on the move, they roamed from job to job as the seasons changed. A man would work for one ranch during the spring roundup, join a trail outfit for the summer, then sign up with another ranch for the fall roundup. When winter came, the ranches laid off a majority of their hands, and most cowboys found themselves without work.

Adventure-seeking young men who went west to become cowboys often were disillusioned. Cowpunching was tougher than they had expected, and not as glamorous. Some greenhorns quit the cowboy trade before a year was up.

A typical cowboy worked at the trade for maybe six or seven years before settling down for good in town or on his own ranch. Only a few men stayed with the job more than ten years. "You never saw an old cowpuncher," a rancher recalled. "They were scarce as hen's teeth. Where they went to, heaven only knows."

Most cowboys were young and single. Still in their late teens or early twenties, they weren't ready to settle down yet. Besides, they didn't earn enough to support a family. Usually they didn't marry until they started ranching for themselves or quit the cattle business altogether.

Some men worked for small family spreads that needed just a few hired hands. Many others were employed by huge outfits supervised by ranch managers and owned by distant corporations with headquarters in the East. Cattle ranching was becoming a big business. There were ranches that covered more land than most New England states. The XIT ranch in Texas occupied parts of ten counties and stretched along two hundred miles of the Texas–New Mexico border. It employed as many as 150 cowboys who rode 1,000 horses, herded 150,000 head of cattle, and branded 35,000 calves every year.

Cowhands employed by small ranches might share the ranch house with the owner and his family. On larger spreads there was always a separate bunkhouse for the hired hands, and perhaps a cookhouse and mess hall as well. The bunkhouse might be little more than a drafty shack with a dirt floor and makeshift bunks for the men's bedrolls. Often it was infested with bedbugs and lice. In warm weather, the men preferred to sleep outside, spreading their bedrolls in wagons or on the ground.

Even on many well-run ranches, there was a raw, unfinished look about the bunkhouse, but it did provide some basic comforts. It had a real wood-plank floor and either a stone fireplace or a big wood-burning stove, where a pot of coffee could be kept warm. The walls might be decorated with postcards, calendars, family photographs, and hand-colored pinups of sedate nineteenth-

The bunkhouse of the O. W. Ranch in Wyoming during the 1880s

century beauties. In the middle of the room, by the stove or fireplace, there was usually a wooden table and a few chairs. Buffalo robes, wolfskins, or heavy woolen blankets covered the bunks. A man was able to store most of his possessions in an old crate under his bunk.

Every cowboy knew that a ranch was set up to tend cows, not to pamper people. Bunkhouse life was simple, at best. The nearest town was a long way off. If a man injured himself or fell ill, he usually had to rely on primitive home remedies.

A sprained ankle might be wrapped in brown paper soaked in

vinegar. A nasty cut was treated with a gummy paste made of chewing tobacco. John Leakey, a Montana cowboy, had a bad accident while building a corral: "I cut my foot nearly in two across the instep with an ax. The boys all went right to work chewing tobacco. Mixing the 'chaw' with flour, they made a poultice for my foot that stopped the bleeding. I rigged up a crutch and went on with my work. The next day I tried to wash the dried flour and tobacco out of the cut, but I couldn't get it all and proud flesh [so-called because of its swelling up] formed in the wound.

"I never had a chance to go to a doctor – but I did stop at old lady Nolan's house one day and show her my foot. It was quite a mess by then, but she gave me some alum, and told me to burn it and put it on the cut to eat the proud flesh out. I followed her instructions and the gash finally healed up. The summer was about gone, though, before I got off that crutch."

On a ranch, as on the trail, a cowboy's day started early. Climbing out of his bunk by the light of a smoky coal oil lamp, the first man up would stoke the fire to take the chill off the morning air. He shaved at the bunkhouse washbasin, pulled on his work clothes, and ambled down to the mess hall for a big breakfast of eggs with ham, sausage, or steak, fresh biscuits or corn bread, and lots of black coffee.

As a rule, cowboys ate their meals silently. Once the food was served, hardly a word was spoken (big talkers were called "leaky mouths"). As soon as a man finished eating, he excused himself and left the table – a habit that had developed on the range, where work was always waiting.

By sunup, all the hands had finished breakfast and wandered over to the corral to catch and saddle their morning horses. The rancher or foreman would assign the day's chores, and the cowboys would ride off. A man might spend the whole day riding the range alone, with no one to talk to but himself and his horse.

In unfenced country, where the cattle grazed freely, they had to be watched to keep them from drifting too far away. A cowboy was always on the lookout for strays. When he found some, he gathered them up and drove them a few miles back to a pasture where good grass and water would encourage them to stay in their home territory.

He also watched for cows that were sick or injured. Any animal with a freshly exposed wound needed to be treated right away for screwworms. Swarms of these wriggling maggots would

Day herders at the XIT Ranch in Texas

quickly infest an open wound, causing a painful infection that could kill the animal. An injured cow had to be roped and thrown so the cowboy could douse its wound with the sticky, smelly screwworm remedy he carried in his saddlebag.

Another chore was pulling cows out of bogholes. The animals became mired as they searched for water or tried to get away from biting insects by wallowing in deep mud. There was only one way to rescue a bogged cow, and that was to get a rope around its neck and pull it free. If the cow had been trapped for a long time, it might be too weak to stand up by itself. More often, the longhorn was fighting mad and would try to charge the man

Getting ready to doctor an ailing steer

who had rescued it as soon as it was dragged to solid ground.

As he rode the range, a cowboy checked on the pastures and the water supply, looking into every spring and water hole. If water holes were clogged with debris, he had to stand in the oozing mud and clean them out with a shovel. In regions where running creeks or spring-fed water holes were scarce, ranches began to build tall windmills to pump water from the ground. When a windmill broke down, which it was likely to do, some unlucky cowboy had to fix it. He would carry his tools and a bucket of grease up a rickety wooden ladder to a precarious platform high above the prairie at the top of the windmill, where he would fiddle with the bearings and gears of the screeching contraption.

During the winter, only the most experienced hands were kept on a ranch's payroll. The rest of the men were laid off for four or five months and told to come back for the spring roundup. A jobless cowboy might rent a room in town, where he would spend the off-season living on his summer earnings, or doing odd jobs like house painting, dishwashing, or bartending.

Some cowhands became "grub-line riders" during the winter: A man would tie his bedroll behind his saddle, climb on his horse, and ride from ranch to ranch doing odd jobs in exchange for free meals and a place to sleep. Towns were so far apart on the western plains that any stranger could ride into a ranch and ask to spend the night. No one was turned away, no matter how poor the ranch or how crowded with guests. Grub-line riders were welcomed at the lonely ranch houses because they carried news and gossip.

Those men who worked on a ranch all winter spent a good part of their time catching up on dull chores like hauling firewood, fixing corrals, mending saddles and harnesses, and repairing wagons and equipment. The most important winter task, however, was to go out on the range from time to time and make sure the cattle were not freezing or starving.

When blizzards swept across the plains, the longhorns turned their tails to the blinding snow and bitter wind and drifted in the same direction the wind was blowing. They might drift miles from their home range. After each storm, cowboys would bundle up in their sheepskin coats, tie bandannas over their ears, and ride out to find the cattle. A good winter horse had to be strong enough to carry a cowboy holding a calf, while at the same time driving a weak cow to a spot where she could feed.

Winter herding

Sometimes a herd was trapped by deep snowdrifts. Shivering and hungry, the animals would stand huddled together, without trying to find food. Cowboys on horseback had to tramp out pathways to hillsides where the wind had blown shallow snow off the grass. Then they led the cattle to these cleared spots. They also had to chop through the ice crust at water holes so the cattle could drink.

At any season, winter or summer, a cowboy might be sent to one of his outfit's remote line camps. Many ranches were far too big to be patrolled from the main cluster of ranch buildings. Line camps were outposts scattered every eight or ten miles around the edges of a ranch. Cowboys stationed at these camps rode along the ranch's boundary lines. They held the cattle on their home range, and if necessary, drove them to better pastures or water holes. They also watched for signs of rustlers, and they hunted or poisoned the wolves and mountain lions that sometimes attacked the livestock.

A line camp was usually a one-room shack built of logs or sod, or a simple dugout carved into the side of a hill, with a crude stone fireplace and a buffalo robe or cowhide hanging at the entrance as a door. If the camp was manned by two cowboys, they would set out in opposite directions every morning and patrol the ranch's boundary until they met the rider coming from the next camp down the line. The men would stop and pass the time of day. Then they would turn around and ride back to their own camps.

Line duty during the winter was the loneliest part of the cowboy's year, especially if he was assigned to a camp by himself. Some men enjoyed the solitude. Jim Christian, a line rider in

*Above:* A line camp on the Matador Ranch in Texas. One cowboy is giving his partner a haircut. *Below:* A line camp on the Pitchfork Ranch in Wyoming. The cowboy at right is saddling up to look for stray cattle after a snowstorm.

Texas, recalled: "When I went into winter camp, I always took plenty of novels and tobacco, and usually a cat. A cat and a briar pipe were lots of company when a fellow spent months shut off from the world. Of course a puncher would drop in for a meal or visit once in a while, or maybe I would meet a puncher now and then while riding; but I have gone for weeks without seeing a soul."

Meanwhile, back at the ranch, evenings at the main bunkhouse weren't all that exciting, either. The men wrote letters, read dime novels, and thumbed through well-worn picture magazines and mail-order catalogs, passing them from hand to hand, then cutting them up so they could paste their favorite pictures on the bunkhouse walls. Over by the stove or the fireplace, a group of regulars might play a few hands of poker or seven-up — perhaps with a lookout posted at the door. On some ranches, card playing or gambling of any kind was strictly forbidden. Most ranches also prohibited liquor. Charles Goodnight, a well-known Texas rancher, had three simple rules for his cowhands: no gambling, no drinking, no fighting.

When cowboys had a day off, they often went hunting for deer, antelope, wild turkeys, or other game. Horse racing was another popular sport. Men from rival ranches would race against each other and compete in games of skill on horseback. A favorite stunt was to lean out of the saddle at full gallop and pick up coins from the ground. The men also held broncobusting and calf-roping contests. These informal competitions eventually spread to the towns as organized rodeos. The earliest rodeos, held as celebrations on the Fourth of July, took place in Deer Trail, Colorado, in 1869; Cheyenne, Wyoming, in 1872; and Pecos,

A cowboy race

Texas, in 1883. The first rodeo trophies were awarded in Prescott, Arizona, on July 4, 1888.

On holidays and other special occasions, a cowhand might have a chance to attend a dance in town or at a local ranch. Dances were the most important social event in the ranching country. They attracted people from all over the county and frequently lasted all night long. For a lonesome bunkhouse cowboy, a dance provided a rare opportunity to meet some lady friends.

Cowboys looked forward to dances for weeks, and when the time came, they dressed up in the best clothes they owned. A man would shine up his silver spurs, put on his white buckskin vest, tie a brilliantly colored silk bandanna around his neck, slick down his hair, and ride twenty miles to attend a dance, even though the men might outnumber the ladies by ten to one. The fiddler played fast and tricky, folks on the sidelines stamped their feet, dancing spurs jingle-jangle-jingled, and the caller shouted: "Ladies in the center, Gents round 'em run, Swing her rope, cowboy, and get yo' one!"

A cowboy's bunk

The barbed-wire fence put an end to the open range.

# The Last of the Old-Time Cowboys

*I'm going to leave old Texas now,*
*For they've got no use for the longhorn cow;*
*They've plowed and fenced my cattle range,*
*And the people there are all so strange.*
*Whoo-a-whoo-a——* ©

THE AMERICAN COWBOY came into his own in Texas during the late 1860s. By the 1890s, the open range roundup and the long trail drive had passed into history, and the cowboy's way of life had changed forever.

Homesteaders had been settling down all over the West. To protect their fields and keep their livestock from straying, they began to use the newly invented barbed wire, which made it possible for the first time to fence off large areas cheaply and easily. Soon, cattle ranchers were also putting up barbed-wire fences. Long strands of barbed wire stretched across the western plains, and wherever the new fences appeared, they marked the end of the open range.

Meanwhile, a network of railroad tracks was spreading throughout the West. By the early 1890s, railroads reached all the way to central Texas, making long trail drives unnecessary. The last herd was driven north to Kansas in 1896.

Barbed-wire fencing brought about great changes in the way beef cattle were raised for market. In the past, during severe winters, large numbers of cattle had starved or frozen on snowbound ranges. The winter of 1886, the worst in human memory, was a disaster for the cattle industry. Hundreds of thousands of longhorns died on the open range, and many prosperous ranchers were wiped out. After that terrible winter, the cattle industry was reorganized.

Cattle no longer wandered freely across the range. Instead, the animals were confined to large fenced pastures, where they could be fed during the winter. Ranchers began to plant and harvest winter feed, which could be hauled out to the cattle whenever necessary. If there were no creeks or water holes within a fenced pasture, windmills were built to pump water from the ground into big tanks, where the cattle could drink.

Inside the newly fenced pastures, ranchers began to develop improved strains of cattle by keeping each breed separate and by controlling what the animals ate. The lean, lanky longhorns with their tough, stringy meat were replaced by Herefords, Durhams, Shorthorns, Brahmans, and other breeds that were easier to raise and yielded higher-quality beef.

Roundups, which once had ranged over hundreds of square miles, now were conducted within barbed-wire enclosures. Men on horseback still drove herds of cattle, but only from their fenced pastures to railroad loading pens a few miles away. Cowboys began to spend much of their time fixing fences, repairing windmills, and mowing hay.

Longhorns were replaced by purebred cattle like these Herefords.

"The range was changing very fast," one rancher remembered. "The old-time range cattle business began to go out of the picture, while fenced pastures and winter feeding and all those modern methods began to look bigger and bigger. Nothing was like it used to be anymore."

The era of the open range cowboy had lasted less than thirty years. Altogether, perhaps twenty-five- or thirty-thousand men

*Above:* Roundups and brandings were conducted within barbed-wire enclosures. *Below:* Fixing a break in the wire fence. Drawing by Frederic Remington.

and boys had gone up the trail. By the time the last trail was closed, those cowboys had captured the imagination of the world.

Ever since the first big trail drives, journalists and other travelers to the West had been writing admiring articles and stories about the rugged Texans who herded half-wild longhorns across the prairies. Eastern writers were fascinated by the cowboy's easy manner in the saddle, by his broad-brimmed hat, his leather chaps, and his big spurs. Many articles and stories presented a glorified and highly exaggerated picture of cowboy life, as in this account from *Leslie's Illustrated*, one of the most widely read magazines of the time: "The cowboy of the great cattle ranges in the West and Southwest is a distinct genus. He is unlike any other being. He enters upon his business life when he is seven years old, and in nine cases out of ten he dies a cowboy, even should he reach the age of Methuselah. His pet is his horse; his toy a revolver; a source of intense pride, his hat — a broad-brimmed straw or wool affair. Leather leggings are worn over his pantaloons, and heavy top boots, with high heels and enormous spurs, protect his feet."

In addition to magazine articles, dime novels were treating millions of avid readers to exciting tales of high adventure in the Wild West. The cowboy heroes in these popular paperbound books were always handsome, brave, and upright. They seemed bigger than life as they galloped across the pages, chasing villains, battling Indians, rescuing maidens in distress. In the industrial cities of the East, in sleepy midwestern towns, on rocky New England farms, teenage boys read these novels by lamplight, then ran away from home to become cowboys themselves. Some of them were willing to work for their "grub" alone — for room and board without wages.

Charles Siringo, who wrote the first of many cowboy memoirs, had "a few words of advice to the young 'tenderfoot' who wishes to become a cow-boy. . . . If you go to work for your 'chuck,' while doing so, work just as hard, and if anything a little harder than if you were getting wages — and at the same time acquire all the knowledge and information possible, on the art of running cattle. Finally one of the Cow Boys on the ranch will quit, or get killed, and you being on hand, will get his place. Or some of the neighboring ranchmen might run short of hands, and knowing of you being out of employment will send after you.

"Your wages will be all the way from $15 up to $40 per month, according to latitude. The further north or northwest you are, the higher your wages will be. . . . After you have mastered the cow business thoroughly — that is, learned how not to dread getting into mud up to your ears, jumping your horse into a swollen stream when the water is freezing, nor running your horse at full speed, trying to stop a stampeded herd, on a dark night, when your course has to be guided by the sound of the frightened steer's hoofs — you command *good* wages, which will be from $25 to $60 per month, according to latitude as I said before."

Siringo's autobiography appeared in 1885. By then, stage plays starring real cowboys and actors dressed as cowboys were thrilling audiences in theatres all over the country. Along with the stage plays, dozens of spectacular live-action shows like Buffalo Bill Cody's Wild West were touring the United States and the capitals of Europe. They featured entire troupes of real cowboys who put on outdoor exhibitions of roping, riding, and broncobusting, and who fought staged battles with bands of real Indians.

The American cowboy was fast becoming a legend. People saw him as a romantic figure, a colorful folk hero on horseback. He was admired for his independent spirit and his free-roaming way of life.

Like all legends, this one was a complex mixture of fact and fancy. The cowboy was in the saddle to herd cows, not to win the West. And yet his work really did demand great daring and skill. Only the best riders and ropers were able to hold down a cowboy's job. It took skill to rope and throw a runaway steer, courage to stay with a stampeding herd. Every cowboy was proud of his tough and dangerous occupation, and of his reputation

Real live cowboys. A roundup crew in Colorado.

Joe Esquival, Jim Kid, Jim Mitchell, Dick Johnson, Billy Bullock, Antonio Esquival, Tom Duffy.
Lying down in front is Johnny Baker, and Billy Johnson.

GROUP OF COWBOYS WITH THE OLD TIME BUFFALO BILL'S WILD WEST SHOW

Show-business cowboys. A group of performers with Buffalo Bill's Wild West Show when it toured Europe in 1888.

Weekend cowboys. Three Dodge City businessmen dressed up as cowboys to have their picture taken around 1885.

as a rugged individualist. He had earned his independence by becoming an expert at his job.

"Cowpunchers were the most independent people on earth," recalled Teddy Blue Abbott. "But if they were independent, they were proud too, and that independence and that pride made for the best results in a cow outfit. To tell the truth, it wasn't thinking about the owner's money that made them so anxious to turn out their herd in good shape. What they cared about was the criticism of the other cowpunchers. They didn't want to hear it said, 'That's a hell of an outfit' — so they made it a point to prove the opposite . . . that their outfit was the best on earth."

The cowboy trade has changed in many ways since the days of the trail drive and the open range. A few of the biggest ranches still run their cattle on ranges covering hundreds of square miles. But on most ranches today, beef cattle are raised and pampered in huge pastures behind fences.

Today's cowboy works with fine breeds of thoroughbred cattle instead of the half-wild longhorn. Often he drives from pasture to pasture in a jeep or pickup truck, hauling his horse behind him in a trailer. Sometimes he flies over the grazing herds at the controls of a helicopter. He lives in a modern bunkhouse where he can watch the latest cowboy films on color television.

Things are different today, yet the cowboy still does almost the same work as his old-time counterpart. He moves herds of cattle from place to place, ropes steers, brands calves, and doctors injured or ailing animals. For all the changes, he remains a jaunty cow herder on horseback.

The old-timers are all dead and gone by now. The pride they felt in being cowboys has become part of their legacy, and part of the American heritage. Sixty years after going up the trail in '79, Teddy Blue said this about the cowboys he had known: "I believe I would know an old cowboy in hell with his hide burnt off. It's the way they stand and walk and talk. There are lots of young fellows punching cows today but they can never take our place, because cowpunching as we knew it is a thing of the past. Riding fence and rounding up pastures ain't anything like the way we used to work cattle in the days of the open range."

Taking things easy

Bibliography
Acknowledgments
Index

A pair of photographs, called a *stereograph*, gave a three-dimensional effect when looked at in a special viewer called a *stereoscope*. Stereographs were very popular in the heyday of the cowboys of the Wild West.

# Bibliography

Abbott, E.C. and Helena Huntington Smith. *We Pointed Them North: Recollections of a Cowpuncher.* Norman: University of Oklahoma Press, 1955.

Adams, Andy. *The Log of a Cowboy.* Boston: Houghton Mifflin Co., 1903.

Brown, Dee. *Trail Driving Days.* New York: Bonanza Books, 1952.

Cook, James H. *Longhorn Cowboy.* Norman: University of Oklahoma Press, 1984.

Dary, David. *Cowboy Culture: A Saga of Five Centuries.* New York: Alfred A. Knopf, Inc., 1981.

Dykstra, Robert R. *The Cattle Towns.* New York: Alfred A. Knopf, Inc., 1968.

Forbis, William H. *The Cowboys.* Alexandria, Virginia: Time-Life Books, 1973.

Haley, J. Evetts. *Charles Goodnight: Cowman and Plainsman.* Boston: Houghton Mifflin Co., 1936.

Horan, James D. *The Great American West.* New York: Crown, 1978.

Hunter, J. Marvin, ed. *The Trail Drivers of Texas*. New York: Argosy-Antiquarian, Ltd., 1963.

Katz, William Loren. *The Black West*. New York: Anchor Books, 1973.

Leakey, John M. *The West That Was: From Texas to Montana*. Lincoln, Nebraska: University of Nebraska Press, 1958.

Lomax, John A. and Alan Lomax. *Cowboy Songs and Other Frontier Ballads*. New York: The Macmillan Company, 1938.

Newark, Peter. *Cowboys*. New York: Exeter Books, 1983.

Rennert, Vincent Paul. *The Cowboy*. New York: Crowell-Collier Press, 1966.

Rounds, Glen. *The Cowboy Trade*. New York: Holiday House, Inc., 1972.

Savage, W. Sherman. *Blacks in the West*. Westport, Conn.: Greenwood Press, 1976.

Savage, William W. Jr. *The Cowboy Hero: His Image in American History and Culture*. Norman: University of Oklahoma Press, 1979.

——————————. *Cowboy Life: Reconstructing an American Myth*. Norman: University of Oklahoma Press, 1975.

Siringo, Charles A. *A Texas Cow Boy or, Fifteen Years on the Hurricane Deck of a Spanish Pony*. Chicago: Siringo and Dobson, 1886.

Taylor, Lonn and Ingrid Maar. *The American Cowboy*. Washington, D.C.: Library of Congress, 1983.

Tyler, Ron. *The Cowboy*. New York: William Morrow and Company, Inc., 1975.

# Acknowledgments

The author gratefully acknowledges permission to quote from the following works:

pages 9 and 47, verses from the preface of the book *Cowboy Songs and Other Frontier Ballads*; page 21 from the song "The Old Chisholm Trail"; page 35 from the song "The Kansas Line"; page 65 from the song "The Wandering Cowboy"; and page 79 from the song "The Texas Song." All these verses are from *Cowboy Songs and Other Frontier Ballads* collected, adapted, and arranged by John A. Lomax and Alan Lomax. TRO–© Copyright 1938 and renewed 1966 Ludlow Music, Inc., New York, N.Y. Used by permission.

pages 18, 19, 26, 53–54, 88 and 89, *We Pointed Them North: Recollections of a Cowpuncher*, by E.C. Abbott and Helena Huntington Smith. New edition copyright 1955 by the University of Oklahoma Press.

pages 30–31 and 33, *Longhorn Cowboy*, by James H. Cook. New edition copyright © 1984 by the University of Oklahoma Press.

page 68, *The West That Was: From Texas to Montana*, by John M. Leakey. © 1958 Southern Methodist University Press. By permission.

page 75, "The Camp Life of a Cowpuncher," by Carroll C. Doshier, Panhandle-Plains Historical Museum, Canyon, Texas. By permission.

Other quoted works:

pages 38, 45, and 62–63, *The Trail Drivers of Texas*, compiled and edited by J. Marvin Hunter. Argosy-Antiquarian, Ltd. New York, 1963.

page 84, *A Texas Cow Boy or, Fifteen Years on the Hurricane Deck of a Spanish Pony*, by Charles A. Siringo. Siringo and Dobson, Publishers. Chicago, 1886.

The photographs and prints in this book are from the following sources and are used with their permission:

Courtesy of The Bancroft Library, University of California: frontis.

Courtesy of the Colorado Historical Society:
pages 36, 64, 85, and 102.

Courtesy of the Denver Public Library, Western History Collection:
pages 11, 20, 22, 23, 25, 72, 74 (bottom), 76, 81, and 82 (bottom).

Courtesy of the Kansas State Historical Society, Topeka:
pages 48 and 87.

Courtesy of the Library of Congress:
pages 12, 13, 30–31, 56, 63, 69, and 92.

Courtesy of the Library of Congress, Erwin E. Smith Collection:
pages 19, 27, 28, 34, 42, 43, 44, 51, 52, 54, 70, 78, and 89.

Courtesy of the Montana Historical Society, Helena:
pages 8 and 60.

Courtesy of the Panhandle-Plains Historical Museum, Canyon, Texas:
pages 37, 46, and 82 (top).

Courtesy of the Western History Collections, University of Oklahoma Library: pages 17 (both), 32, 39, 50, 59, 62, 74 (top), and 86.

Courtesy of the Archives-American Heritage Center, University of Wyoming:
pages 67 and 77.

# Index

Page numbers in *italics* refer to captions

Abbott, Teddy Blue, 18, 19, 26, 54, 88, 89
Abilene, Kansas, 16, 61

Barbed wire, use of, *78*, 79, 80, *82*
Bedrolls, 10, 37, *50*, 51, 55, 66
Beef
   market for, 13-14
   not eaten on trail drives, 51
Blizzards, 72-73
Branding, 34, 40, 41, *42-43*, 44, *82*
Broncobusting, *30-31*, 31-33, *32*
Buffalo, 14
Buffalo Bill Cody's Wild West Show, 84-85, *86*
Bunkhouses, *66-67*, *77*, 88
Burrows, G.O., 62-63

Cattle, purebred, 80, *81*
Cattle country, 14, *15*
Cattle ranch on Cimarron River, *64*
Cattle-raising industry, 14
   modern, 88
   reorganization of, 80, *81*
Chaps (*chaparreras*), 22-23
Cherokee Light Brigade, 59
Cherokee Outlet (Oklahoma), *17*
Cheyenne, Wyoming, 75
Chicago, 14, 61
Chisholm Trail, *15*, 48
Christian, Jim, 73-75
Chuck boxes, 50, *52*
Chuck wagons, 36, 37, 38, *39*, 45, 49-51, *50*, 53
   contents of, on the trail, 49-50
Cimarron River, *64*

Civil War, 12, 13, 16
Clothes and equipment, cowboy,
    20-33, 22
  bandannas, 24
  boots, 23-24
  chaps, 22-23
  dressing up, 26
  firearms, 18, 26-27
  hats, 24-26, 28
  horses, 29-33
  lariats, 11, 20, 27-28
  saddles, 28-29
  spurs, 24, 25
Colorado, 14, 36, 61
Comanches (Indians), 60-61
Cook, James, 30, 33
Cooks, 9, 37, 38, 40, 51-52, 55
  importance of, 49
Cow hunts, 14
Cowboy race, 76
Cowboy Songs and Other Frontier
    Ballads, 9, 47
Cowboys, 8, 9-10, 12, 16-19
  blacks, 16, 17
  clothes and equipment, 20-33
  food, 37, 39-40, 50, 51, 68
  grub-line riders, 71
  guns used by, 18, 26-27
  hard life of, 18-19
  Indians (Native Americans), 16,
    17
  Mexicans, 16
  necessary skills of, 85-88

nineteenth-century tales and leg-
    ends, 83-85
  number of old-time, 81-83
  origin of, 10-12
  photographs, 8, 10, 12, 17, 19,
    20, 22, 23, 25, 28, 85, 87, 92
  pride of, in their jobs, 88-89
  today's, 88
  wandering, 65-66
  winter layoffs from ranches, 71
  youth of, general, 9, 65-66
  see also Ranches, cattle; Round-
    ups; Trail drives
Cowpokes (or cowpunchers), ori-
    gin of names, 60
Craig, Hiram, 38, 45
Cutting out, 2, 40-41

Dakotas, 14, 47
Dances, 76
Day herders at XIT Ranch, 69
Deer Trail, Colorado, 75
Doctoring and ailing steer, 70
Dodge City, Kansas, 17, 19, 61, 62,
    87
Drag riders, 53-54
Dust, trail, 53-54

Fenders, 29
Flankers, 41, 42-43
Food, 37, 39-40, 50, 51, 68

Games and amusements, 36
Goodnight, Charles, 75
Goodnight-Loving Trail, *15*, 60-61
Grigsby, J.M., 57

Haircut, *74*
Hale County, Texas, *46*
Herron, Jim, 57-58
(Hickok), Wild Bill, 18
Horse wranglers, 9, 37, 38, *39*, *46*,
    49, 52-53
Horses, 29-33
    broncobusting, *30-31, 31-33, 32*
    mustangs, 30-31
    special abilities of, 33, 40
    *see also* Remudas

Indian Territory (Oklahoma), 16,
    58, 59
Indians, 10, 19, 30, 47, 49
    attacks by, along the trails, 59-
        60, 61
    Caddo or Kickapoo, *17*
    Cherokees, 59
    Comanches, 60
    as cowboys, 16, *17*
    tolls demanded from trail driv-
        ers, 58-61

Kansas, 10, 14, 26, 47, 61, 62, 80
Kansas City, Missouri, 14, 61
"Kansas Line, The," 35

Lariats (*la reata*), 11, 20, 27-28
Leakey, John, 68
*Leslie's Illustrated*, 83
Levis, 21
Line camps and line duty, 73-75,
    *74*
Longhorn cattle, 9-10, 12, *13-14*
    alignment on the trail, 53
    care of, during blizzards, 72-73
    free-roaming, 35
    loading aboard stockcars, *60*
    replaced by purebreds, 80, *81*
    a scary lot, 57
    on the trail, *46*
    treating sick and injured, 69-71,
        *70*
    value of, 47

Masterson, Bat, 18
Matador Ranch, Texas, *74*
Mexico, 10
Miles City, Montana, *8*
Montana, *8*, 14, 47
    Territory, *46*
Moving camp, *50*

New Mexico, 60, 66

Ogallala, Nebraska, 19
Oklahoma, 16, *17*
"Old Chisholm Trail, The," 21

Open range, end of, *78*, *79*
O.W. Ranch, Wyoming, *67*

Pecos, Texas, 75-76
Pitchfork Ranch, Wyoming, *74*
Prescott, Arizona, 76

Railroads, growth of, 79-80
Ranches, cattle, 65-76
  a big business, 66
  blizzards, cattle care during, 72-
    73, *74*
  bogholes, pulling cows from, 70-
    71
  chores, 69-71
  dances, 76
  early rising and breakfast, 68
  evening activities, 75
  home remedies, 67-68
  line camps and line duty, 73-75,
    *74*
  living quarters, 66-*67*, 77
  no pampering, 67
  off-duty relaxations, 75-76
  sick and injured cows, 69-71
  water holes and windmills,
    checking, 71
  winter chores, 71-72
  winter layoffs, 71
  Red River, *58*

Remudas, *37*, *38*, *40*, *46*, *49*, *53*
  roping a horse from, *37-38*
Rodeos, beginnings of, 75-76
Roping a calf, *27*, *41*, *42-43*
  cow protecting roped calf, *42*
Roundups, 35-45
  branding new calves, *34*, *40*, *41*,
    *42-43*, *44*
  camps, *25*, 36-38
  crew in Colorado, *85*
  cutting out, *2*, 40-41
  enclosed, 80, *82*
  notching ears, 44
  preparations, 35-36
  rounding up, actual, 38-39
  roundup boss as judge, 45
  sorting out, 40, 45
  tallying, 40

Saddles, *10*, *11*, *21*, *28-29*
San Antonio, Texas, 62
Shawnee Trail, *15*, 59
Show-business cowboys, *86*
Singing on trail drives, importance
  of, 55-57
Siringo, Charles, 84
Sleeping outdoors, *102*
Stampedes, *10*, *27*, *33*, *47*, 57-58
  dangers to cowboys, 58
  man-originated, 14
Stereographs and stereoscopes, *92*
Stirrups, 23, 29

Taking things easy, *89*
Texas, *8, 9*, 12, 13, 14, 16, *17*, 26,
    47, 58, 60, 62, 66, *69*, 80
    Panhandle, *17*
"Texas Song, The," 79
Trail bosses, 9, 48-49, 53, 54, 57,
    59
Trail-drivers, *8, 9*
    positions of, 53-54
Trail drives, 9-10, 18, 47-63
    crossing Indian lands, 58-61
    earnings on, 62
    end of the trail, *61-63*
    hazards of, 47-48
    joy at end of trail, 61
    night guard, 55, *56*
    participants in, 48-52
    river crossings, 58, *59*
    singing, calming effect of, 55, 57
    stampedes, 57-58

trails north from Texas, *15*, 48,
    59, 60-61
    typical activity on, 52-55
Trail herds, 9, *46*, 48, 52, 53, 54,
    55

Vaqueros, 10-12, *11*

"Wandering Cowboy, The," 65
Weekend cowboys, *87*
Wichita, Kansas, 61
Windmills, 71, 80
Winter herding, *72*
Wranglers. *See* Horse wranglers
Wyoming, 14, 47, *67, 74*

XIT Ranch, Texas, *8*, 66

Even at the ranch, cowboys sometimes preferred to sleep outdoors.

# About the Author

Russell Freedman says that like other youngsters of his generation, he "became a 'cowboy' at an early age," when he was growing up in San Francisco in the 1930s. He thought a cowboy was a "fellow who says 'yup' and 'nope,' who never complains, who shoots straight, and whose horse comes when he whistles."

Years later, when Mr. Freedman started research for this book, he found that many of his ideas were not borne out by the facts. But he admires the real cowboys, and he loved writing about them. He selected the photos and prints for the book from the archives in seven western states and the Library of Congress.

Russell Freedman was born in San Francisco where he began his writing career as a reporter for the The Associated Press. He now lives in New York City. Mr. Freedman has written over thirty books on subjects ranging from animal behavior to American history. His 1983 book *Children of the Wild West* won the Western Heritage Award given by the National Cowboy Hall of Fame and was selected as an ALA Notable Children's Book.

## DATE DUE

| NOV 18 2019 | | | |
|---|---|---|---|
| | | | |
| | | | |
| | | | |
| | | | |
| | | | |
| | | | |
| | | | |
| | | | |
| | | | |
| | | | |
| | | | |
| | | | |
| | | | |
| | | | |
| | | | |
| | | | |
| | | | |
| GAYLORD | | | PRINTED IN U.S.A. |